SHAPED BY SCRIPTURE

Live by Faith

ROMANS 1-7

DOUG WARD

Copyright © 2024 by The Foundry Publishing®
The Foundry Publishing
PO Box 419527
Kansas City, MO 64141
thefoundrypublishing.com

978-0-8341-4290-9

Cover Design: J. R. Caines
Interior Layout: Jeff Gifford

The internet addresses, email addresses, and phone numbers in this book are accurate at the time of publication. They are provided as a resource. The Foundry Publishing does not endorse them or vouch for their content or permanence.

Contents

THE *SHAPED BY SCRIPTURE* SERIES

The first step of an organized study of the Bible is the selection of a biblical book, which is not always an easy task. Often people pick a book they are already familiar with, books they think will be easy to understand, or books that, according to popular opinion, seem to have more relevance to Christians today than other books of the Bible. However, it is important to recognize the truth that God's Word is not limited to just a few books. All the biblical books, both individually and collectively, communicate God's Word to us. As Paul affirms in 2 Timothy 3:16, "All Scripture is God-breathed and is useful for teaching, rebuking, correcting and training in righteousness." We interpret the term "God-breathed" to mean inspired by God. If Christians are going to take 2 Timothy 3:16 seriously, then we should all set the goal of encountering God's Word as communicated through all sixty-six books of the Bible. New Christians or those with little to no prior knowledge of the Bible might find it best to start with a New Testament book like 1 John, James, or the Gospel of John.

By purchasing this volume, you have chosen to study the first half of the book of Romans, which is considered by some to be Paul's greatest theological treatise. This epistle heavily emphasizes the reign of Christ and the role of faith in a believer's life.

How This Study Works

This Bible study is intended for a period of seven weeks. We have chosen a specific passage for each week's study. This study can be done individually or with a small group.

For individual study, we recommend a five-day study each week, following the guidelines given below:

1 On the first day of the study, read the relevant passage several times until you become fully familiar with the verses, words, and phrases.

2 On the second day, we will review the setting and organization of the passage.

3 On the third day, we will observe some of the realities portrayed in the passage.

4 On the fourth day, we will investigate the relationship of the individual passage to the larger story of God in the Bible.

5 On the fifth day, we will reflect on the function of the story as we hear it today, the invitation it extends to us, and our response to God, who speaks through God's Word.

If this Bible study is done as a group activity, we recommend that members of the group meet together on the sixth day to share and discuss what they have learned from God's Word and how it has transformed their lives.

You may want to
have a study Bible to
give you additional
insights as we work
through the book
of Romans. Other
helpful resources
are *Discovering the
New Testament* and
the New Beacon
Bible Commentary
volumes *Romans 1-8*
and *Romans 9-16*,
available from The
Foundry Publishing.

Literary Forms in the Bible

There are several literary forms represented throughout the Bible. The divinely inspired writers used various techniques to communicate God's Word to their ancient audiences. The major literary forms (also known as genres) of the Bible are:

- narratives

- laws

- history

- Wisdom literature (in the form of dialogues and proverbial statements)

- poetry (consisting of poems of praise, lament, trust in God, and more)

- prophecy

- discourses

- parables

- miracle stories

- letters (also known as epistles)

- exhortations

- apocalyptic writings

Within each of these forms, one may find subgenres. Each volume in the *Shaped by Scripture* series will briefly overview the genres found in the book of the Bible that is the subject of that study.

When biblical writers utilized a particular literary form, they intended for it to have a specific effect on their audience. This concept can be understood by examining genres that are familiar to us in our contemporary setting. For example, novels that are comedies inspire good and happy feelings in their readers; tragedies, on the other hand, are meant to induce sorrow. What is true of the intended effect of literary forms in contemporary literature is also true of literary forms found in the Bible.

THE BOOK OF ROMANS

The book of Romans is part of a larger collection of thirteen New Testament letters that have been attributed to the apostle Paul. The authorship of six of these letters is debated to some extent today. Three (1 Timothy, Titus, and 2 Thessalonians) are considered by many scholars to be doubtful in their connection to Paul. Three others (Colossians, Ephesians, and 2 Timothy) are disputed by some, although the trend is swinging back toward Pauline authorship. The seven that remain (Galatians, 1 and 2 Corinthians, Romans, 1 Thessalonians, Philippians, and Philemon) are widely considered to be undisputed letters from the hand of Paul.

Among these seven letters, Romans clearly stands apart. Paul's letter to the church in Rome is the jewel of Pauline literature. It is the letter where we see the most complete expression of Pauline theology and practice. In it we can see the depth and breadth of Paul's thought and his deep concern for this new faith.

In most of his letters, Paul is responding to an ongoing issue in the church to whom the letter is written. Sometimes that local church has written to Paul with a list of questions they have about congregational problems or theological issues (see 1 Corinthians). In other letters, Paul is emotionally responding to a sudden crisis that needs his immediate attention (see Galatians). In still others, Paul is writing a personal letter to a person he knows well (see Philemon).

None of these reasons for writing are present in Romans. In this letter Paul is writing to a church he did not start and has never visited in person but would like to visit in the near future. He wants to introduce himself to the church and allow the church to get to know him and the gospel message he proclaims. In Romans, Paul has time to think about what is important, so he takes his time and presents his argument in a lengthy and orderly fashion.

Romans, more than any other letter, is a glimpse into the mind and theology of Paul. Perhaps for this reason, Romans has always been a highly important New Testament work, especially for those in the Protestant world. Martin Luther considered Romans to be the central part of the New Testament, while John Calvin said it opened a gateway for the rest of the Bible. John Wesley was reading Luther's "Preface to Romans" when he felt his heart strangely warmed. It would not be an exaggeration to say that Romans has been the most influential book in the New Testament when it comes to the theology of the church. Within the pages of this letter, one finds the problem of humanity explained, God's response to the problem we created, and how the Christian life is to be lived. Romans is Paul's thorough presentation of what it means to be a Christian.

Who Wrote Romans?

Romans was undeniably written by the apostle Paul. When some people think about Paul, they have an image of this leader of the early church confidently advising these young congregations in a difficult environment. The biggest problem with that view is that Paul was never recognized as a leader of the early church. He openly flouted the rules and expectations of the leadership of the church in Jerusalem. As a result, Jerusalem's leadership never trusted him, and some in the Jewish wing of the early Christian church actively opposed his efforts. To them, Paul was a dangerous presence, opening the church to gentiles without requiring them to fully observe the Jewish requirements.

Many believers today fail to appreciate how difficult the battle was for Paul. Before his encounter with Christ on the road to Damascus, he spent considerable time and energy persecuting the first Jewish believers in the early church. His motive was to keep the Jewish faith pure and the synagogue free from controversy and improper belief. Proclaiming that a crucified Jesus was their Messiah was intolerable for Saul. After his dramatic experience on the Damascus road, Paul changed his stripes and tried to integrate with the early church. Understandably, those efforts did not go well. Few were willing to trust a former leading persecutor of the church. He eventually found an ally in the church at Antioch—a congregation that accepted Paul, befriended him, supported his ministry, and sent him on his missionary journeys.

Early in his ministry, he was on the opposite side of the question of gentile inclusion from Peter and James. Paul passionately believed gentiles could be full participants in the new faith without being required to observe Jewish customs. Paul's biggest challenge was in trying to convince the early church to trust him and not James, the very *brother* of Jesus, or Peter, Jesus's own disciple. The fact that so many of Paul's letters remain demonstrate to us that his view eventually carried the day, but in the first century, the issue was very much in doubt.

Although the issue was murky in the collective opinion of the early church, it was exceedingly clear to Paul. Jesus commanded his followers to make disciples of every nation. "Every nation" includes gentiles! Requiring new believers to become Jewish first would make Jesus's command meaningless, and the early church would never have become "Christianity" but would have remained a faction of Judaism forever. The tension between Jewish and gentile Christianity persisted throughout Paul's entire ministry, but it was not the only tension the early church experienced. These early believers existed within the larger Roman Empire. The largest and most powerful nation the world had ever known was at the height of its power and influence in the first century, and Rome was its capital city. To reach the world that existed then, Christians in Rome would need a thriving local church that directed people to Christ. Paul wanted his influence to be known in that church.

Paul's Background

There are a few things it is helpful to know about Paul's background so we understand him better. Paul spent the first half of his life zealously pursuing the Judaism of his youth in the city of Tarsus, which was famous for being the city where Marc Antony and Cleopatra joined forces and launched a civil war against Rome. As a result, Rome kept a permanent garrison of soldiers in Tarsus so no other rebellions could begin there. As a youth, Paul went to Jerusalem to train under Gamaliel, who was the grandson of the famed Rabbi Hillel. Paul's intensity, zeal, and effort were noticed, and according to his own account in Philippians, he quickly rose through the ranks of the Pharisees. As a young man, his role was to teach established Jewish doctrine and to correct any incorrect teaching he encountered. Paul's role was limited to the synagogues, which was precisely where he began to encounter the strange and new teachings about a resurrected Messiah.

In spite of what we do know about Paul and his background, we still have questions about what we don't know, and several incorrect assumptions about him have also been made.

One question we have regards how Paul became a Roman citizen. Rome did not hand out citizenship indiscriminately to just anyone, so it is a surprise to see this status bestowed on Paul. The most likely explanation is that Paul was a citizen because his father was. We know Paul was a tentmaker, a trade he would have learned from his father. In Tarsus, a city with an army garrison, it seems plausible that Paul's father could have received Roman citizenship as a reward for making tents for the Roman army. Next, it is reasonable to assume that the child who zealously studied Judaism either helped his father make these tents, or accompanied him to deliver them to the army, or both. We can logically conclude Paul would, in the course of these activities, have made profitable and useful contacts with key members of the army—enough to eventually be rewarded with citizenship in the same way his father was.

One incorrect assumption about Paul is that he traveled around to kill Christians. Paul's authority was valid only within Jewish synagogues. His position was within the power structures of the Jewish religious leaders, not within the power structures of Rome. Rome and Rome alone wielded the power of capital punishment. In fact, if someone wanted to find themselves on a cross, the easiest way to accomplish it would be to go around killing people without Rome's authority. This knowledge still leaves us wondering what Paul was doing in Acts 7 at the stoning of Stephen. Some assume that Paul has ordered the public execution, but that detail is nowhere in the story. We only know that he was there and that he approved of the violent action. Of course, Saul would've disagreed strongly with Stephen's proclamations that Jesus had died and risen again and that he should now be considered the Son of God. This teaching, perceived as heretical by the Jews who did not believe in Jesus, was popping up in more and more places, including in the synagogue at Damascus. Therefore, Paul set out on a journey toward Damascus, where he planned to correct the teaching in that synagogue. As we know, he unexpectedly met the risen Christ while on this very journey.

Another incorrect assumption people have made about Paul is that he changed his name from Saul to Paul after he encountered Jesus, but that is not true. A Roman citizen of that time was known by a tribal—or ethnic—name, a Roman name, and a birthplace. Paul, therefore, was Saulus Paulus of Tarsus. When Paul is in Jerusalem early in the book of Acts, he is simply known as Saul. When he starts his missionary travels, he is known by his Romanized name of Paul—as one would expect in the far reaches of the Roman Empire. Later in Acts, when Paul returns to Jerusalem, we find the name Saul being used again. Even though he spent his early life as a zealous and committed Jew, Paul was very much a man of two worlds. It would be hard to comprehend anyone better suited for the task of proclaiming a Jewish savior to a Roman (i.e., gentile) world.

Literary Form

Romans, like the other Pauline literature in the New Testament, is a letter, but the subject matter is so widespread that it lacks the focus of a personal letter, or of one like Galatians that targets a specific issue. Even so, there are well-recognized traits of an ancient letter in Romans. The usual epistolary greeting is prominent, as is the concluding section filled with personal notes and greetings. Romans also probably has the most noted *paraenesis* of the New Testament letters. A *paraenesis* is the section of a letter where the writer gives practical advice on how to respond based on what is presented in the main body of the letter. Romans 12–14 is a wonderful example of a *paraenesis*.

In recent years scholars have noted the presence and importance of a style known as diatribe within Paul's letter to the Romans. When we hear that word today, we often imagine an intense argument or a scuffle between two opponents. In ancient rhetoric, however, this word is used differently. In Romans, Paul is often arguing not with a specific opponent but against anticipated objections to his statements. His effective use of rhetorical diatribe shows that he is engaged in an important teaching dialogue

10

with Christian Jews and gentiles about this new faith that is connected to Judaism but also stands apart in many critical ways.

The reader of Romans should also be aware of blocks of material that thematically connect. Romans 1–3, 5–8, and 9–11 are examples of sections that need to be read as a larger block of material and understood together.

Date

Paul's ministry centered around three missionary journeys he made across the Roman Empire. The last of these journeys is often called his "letter-writing journey," from 54–57 CE. Romans was written close to the culmination of Paul's missionary efforts. While the precise date is difficult to decipher and unnecessary to pinpoint exactly, it is important to see that it comes after years of reflection and active ministry. Many scholars suppose that Paul wrote this letter from Corinth because he stopped there for roughly three months during his final missionary journey (see Acts 20:3). Since he was in the middle of this journey, most scholars place the writing of Romans around 56 CE, by which time Paul had been planting churches and traveling for ten years. He was well into his ministry and had already experienced and suffered much. In Corinth, Paul had time to reflect on what was important and what would help the vital church congregation in Rome. He also had ample time to write without being pressured by a crisis. This letter was a great occasion for Paul to be both timely and thorough.

Entering the Story

The previous decade had been a busy and impactful one for Paul. His message of the gospel was spreading around the world in ways he could not have anticipated. He never fully gained the trust of the church in Jerusalem, so he began his journeys from the church in Antioch. His message was not usually welcome among Jewish believers in the synagogues, where he always went first, but he found success with the gospel among the gentiles. Maybe the most surprising thing about Paul's life is how this man who started out as a zealous Pharisee eventually became the force that spread the gospel to the non-Jewish world.

Paul's first journey was spent preaching the gospel throughout Asia Minor, which is modern-day Turkey. This was the first place the gentiles responded, and it led directly to the Jerusalem Conference to settle the issue of whether gentiles would be allowed in the church. Paul followed that journey with a second missionary journey a year later, during which he and the young physician Luke started churches in Europe in places like Philippi, Thessalonica, and Corinth.

Paul was especially intrigued by Corinth. He ended up staying there for eighteen months and started a thriving, albeit troubled church there. The reason Corinth was so attractive was its cosmopolitan nature. It was a thriving crossroads of trade, tourism, and Roman culture. If one wanted to spread the message of the gospel, there were not many places better than Corinth.

In the middle of his third journey, Paul had returned to Corinth, the familiar place where he had spent such a productive year and a half a few years earlier. As Paul rested in Corinth, he thought about the gospel and about how the church could grow. If the message of the gospel were ever to spread like wildfire, Paul knew Rome was the key. As the capital of this vast empire, everything connected in Rome. If the church could gain a strong foothold in Rome, then anything was possible. As Paul sat in Corinth, he knew he had to get to Rome. I don't know if Paul had a concrete plan, but he trusted he would make it there eventually. He had heard there were Christians in Rome, but it was a church he did not start. However, he would need to use the church as a base if he ever made it to Rome. Paul did not want to be a stranger there if and when he did make it to Rome, so he decided to write a letter to introduce himself and to give the church in Rome his understanding of the gospel. This would not be like his letters to other churches. This would be a letter worthy of the capital of the great empire.

Since Paul was not responding to an immediate crisis, he decided to take his time with this letter, explaining the new faith to the church located in the most vital city of the first century. Paul had already spent so much time thinking through this faith in the previous years. The letter to the church in Rome would be a great opportunity to present his gospel in a measured, systematic fashion. He wanted to prevent the divide between Jewish and gentile believers that plagued other churches. More importantly, he desired to explain how sin impacts everyone and how Christ is the answer for both groups—but he wouldn't stop there. Paul wanted to talk on an individual level about how sin diminishes each person, how Christ redeems us, and how the Spirit empowers us to triumph in the midst of a powerful empire and the inevitable hardships to come.

Historical Context

In the first century, Rome was the dominant power in the Western world. From modern-day Scotland in the north to the Sahara Desert in the African south, and from Spain in the west all the way to the Euphrates in the east, Rome reigned supreme. There was no rival power, and the first century was the pinnacle of Roman strength.

A few years before Paul's letter to the Romans was written, Emperor Claudius had evicted the Jews from Rome in 49 CE. There is a degree of uncertainty about why the

Jews were expelled, but an ancient reference in Suetonius points toward friction with the new Christian believers as a potential cause. Since Christianity would have still been viewed as part of Judaism, the Jews were ordered to leave the capital city.

After the expulsion of the Jews, any remaining Christians in Rome would have been gentile believers unaffected by the decree, which led to significant changes in the church. The Jewish believers would have been the older and more established adherents, and now they were gone, along with the Jewish sensibilities and requirements. The church in Rome had become entirely gentile as a result of the decree. After the death of Claudius, a new emperor named Nero assumed power and reversed the Jewish eviction, bringing the Jews back into Rome five years after their expulsion. The Jewish Christians returned to a changed church where they were no longer dominant. If the gospel was going to spread in Rome, the church could not be divided along ethno-cultural lines.

The dividing lines between Jews and gentiles were not arbitrary. These two groups of people had distinct histories and saw the world in vastly different ways. The Jews had a long and unique history of being subject to a number of conquering empires, of which Rome was simply the latest. They saw themselves as a people who were called to have a special relationship with the one true God, who required certain rules and regulations to be followed. This belief served to craft a unique identity for the Jews, but those same requirements had also led to Jewish isolation from the people around them. To maintain their status as chosen people, Jews believed they must observe the requirements of the law and worship the one they called the God of Israel. Other nations had their own gods, which Jews acknowledged as reality, but they viewed the worship of these other gods as idolatry even when those nations were more powerful. Nearly all of the earliest Christians were Jews and, due to their unique identity, continued to observe the traditional historical Jewish requirements. Paul's ministry to the gentiles was slowly changing the church, but the differences between the groups remained. The Jewish requirements that isolated them as a people tended to have the same consequence in the church.

The looming presence of Rome as the most powerful kingdom the world had ever seen was obviously a factor in the life of the budding church. It is hard for us to comprehend how powerful and pervasive Rome was. Their control and power were unquestioned, and they enforced peace with an iron fist. Along with the negative aspects of such great power also came great innovation. Rome built roads throughout the empire, making extensive travel possible for the first time. The world now also had a unified system and a universal written language, Koine Greek. In our modern world, a great number of people learn English in addition to their native languages. English, mostly because of the far-reaching, long-lasting influence of the British Empire, has become the language of commerce and diplomacy. In Rome, Koine Greek served the same purpose. We look at Rome with warranted negativity, but their powerful position created unique conditions for the far-flung spread of the gospel.

The Jews resented the power of Rome, but it did come with an enforced peace. Rome installed Herod to rule over the Jews, thinking they would welcome one of their own in power, but that was not the result. Herod was never accepted and was always treated with suspicion, even though he remained in power for more than thirty years.

As Paul sat down to write his letter to the Romans, there were changes happening in the empire. Nero was new to the throne, having assumed power in 54 CE at the age of sixteen. Nero was popular during the early years of his reign, although a number of prominent people began to die at the direction of his mother, Agrippina. It is hard to say what was known at this point. It is possible that those with discerning eyes could see trouble brewing. This trouble might endanger the young church that inhabited the populous city. It was easy to see that, whatever happened, the church in Rome would be front and center to witness it. That is why Paul wrote to this potentially influential church. Incredibly, the letter Paul wrote to them is still relevant today.

Context of the Letter

Paul's letter to the Romans reflects the world in which he lived, not the world we modern readers inhabit. Nor should it be read through the eyes of Martin Luther, John Calvin, or any other figure from the years between Paul and now. Paul wrote to a real church in the middle of a definite period of history. We should always be careful to keep that place and time in mind as we read. If we fail to do so, we run the risk of making Romans say what we want it to say, instead of what Paul meant it to say. We should always remember that all of our New Testament is anchored in history and a specific place and time. The first readers collected, saved, and copied these letters because of how the words applied to their place and time.

As Paul writes Romans, he is always thinking about the people who comprise the church. There are places in Romans where Paul writes specifically to the gentiles, addressing concerns that are unique to them. At other times he turns his attention to the Jews, correcting attitudes and actions that flow from their unique history. Eventually he writes to the entire church about the sinful condition we all share and about the remedy that is found in Christ. In these passages we find some of the most familiar and deeply loved sections of the New Testament.

Paul closes his letter on a triumphant note, grounding the answer to sin not only in the death and resurrection of Jesus but also in the ongoing and indwelling presence of the Holy Spirit. Paul describes an active, living faith. Since our faith is living, we can live in a way that makes a difference in our world. This is the triumph of Romans.

This letter is not a theoretical exercise for Paul but real advice he is offering on how Christ followers can live and respond in a world that is far from ideal. We should remember the reality of life in Rome under Nero as we read Paul's advice on how to live with governing authorities that do not share Christian sensibilities. There are times when those in the modern world think we are facing a unique problem in history. The letter to the Romans should remind us that the church and Christians have already seen it all. For this and many other reasons, Romans is as relevant and fresh today as it was in the first century. Now is a great time to read Romans from the perspective of history and, in so doing, discover the ways it still speaks powerfully to Christians today.

Major Theological Themes

Romans, as Paul's most extensive and systematic treatise about God and this new faith that eventually came to be called Christianity, is rich with theological themes we will explore together over the next few weeks.

Jesus is the Son of God; the Roman emperor is not.

The gospel of Jesus Christ is for everyone—Jewish and non-Jewish alike as well as any other identities humans might use to divide themselves.

Being a child of God is about following Christ by faith, not by works.

When the people of God act in ways that are contrary to the love of God, we make a mockery of the name of God, and the world distrusts God.

God's faithfulness cannot be undone or nullified by humanity's unfaithfulness.

Hope in God is only possible when we accept that the promises of God can only be enacted *by* God—and not by our own effort.

Christ's incarnation, death, and resurrection on our behalf are definitive proof that God loves us.

The power of sin is not as powerful as the grace of God.

We are able to make a choice about whether we will be mastered by sin or by God.

Holiness is about character more than actions. Holy character will result in holy action.

ROMANS 1

Rome was the most powerful political force in the first-century world. If the early church was going to impact the larger culture, it would have to be a viable presence in Rome. There was a new church in Rome that was made up of gentiles and Jewish Christians returning from exile (see the Historical Context section in the Introduction to the Book of Romans chapter for more information on the Jewish expulsion from Rome). Paul's wish was for the church to be a unified body of believers. For that to happen, the gentiles needed to respect the unique history of the Jews, and the Jewish Christians needed to welcome the gentiles into fellowship. Paul writes to both groups in an effort to unite them.

There is a larger issue here in Romans. If the gospel was going to spread into the larger culture, Paul wanted to be sure that the message that got spread was that gentiles *and* Jews come to Christ through simple faith. No group had an inside track or secret entrance. He also wanted to be sure the wider Roman world realized the depths to which humanity had fallen. Whether it was an unjust emperor on the throne, violent soldiers marching through a town, or harsh words from a neighbor, the real culprit behind all of it was sin. The good news for all—Jews and gentiles, slaves and the free—is that Christ is the remedy for the shared problem of sin and that there is another way to live, animated by the Holy Spirit.

WEEK 1, DAY 1

Absorb the passage in Romans 1 by reading it aloud several times until you become familiar with its verses, words, and phrases.

WEEK 1, DAY 2

The Setting

The apostle Paul was on another journey, and he was currently stationed in Corinth for a multiple-month stay. As he looked at the cosmopolitan setting of Corinth, he began to ponder how much good the gospel might be able to do in a city as important and vital as Rome. He had heard the news about the gospel taking root in Rome and wanted to ensure that the new church growing in Rome understood good doctrine and practice so they could represent and practice Christianity well. The best way he knew to make that happen was by writing a letter to this new church. Paul took his time and organized his thoughts.

The Message

Paul wanted to begin by addressing the condition of the world. Although the larger world was definitely on his mind, this chapter really was for the gentiles. We know this for two reasons. First, the overwhelming majority of people in Rome would have been gentiles, as would almost all of the citizens in the vast Roman Empire. Second, Paul directly addressed the Jewish Christians in Romans 2. By directly addressing each group's unique circumstances, Paul was speaking to both parts of the Roman church in describing the state of the world. To a first-century Jewish Christian mind, the world was made up entirely of Jew and gentile—there were no other categories. Paul began by letting the gentiles know why the world was not ideal, while also explaining the role they played in the downward spiral.

To discover the message of Romans 1, let's divide the passage into its four major sections. **Summarize or paraphrase the general message or theme of each section (following the pattern provided).**

1. Romans 1:1–7
This is a customary introduction and initial greeting in an ancient letter.

What else do you see in these verses besides salutations?

2. Romans 1:8–17

3. Romans 1:18–24

4. Romans 1:25–32

WEEK 1, DAY 3

What's Happening in the Passage?

As we read through these passages there are certain ideas and words that were familiar to the original readers but are not as familiar to us. Two thousand years and a vastly different culture obscure some of these ideas from us today. You may encounter some of these words and ideas in your study today. Some of them have been explained in more detail in the **Word Study Notes** below. If you want even more detail you can supplement this study with a Bible dictionary or commentary.

1. Romans 1:1–7

This section represents a traditional beginning of a Greco-Roman letter and is the part called the salutation. A salutation will announce who the letter is from as well as the letter's intended audience. The traits that set this salutation apart from traditional ancient salutations are in verses 2–6, where Paul briefly writes about the Jewish roots of the gospel, the resurrection of Jesus, the presence of the Spirit, and the inclusion of the gentiles. Somewhat like an abstract in an academic paper, Paul has summarized here in his opening all the subjects he intends to discuss in detail throughout the letter. Paul also twice declares Jesus the Son of God in this opening.[1]

2. Romans 1:8–17

In most ancient Roman letters, the salutation is followed by a thanksgiving section, and Romans is no different. Paul wants his readers to know how much he loves and prays for them, and how deeply he desires to visit them. In verse 14, Paul transitions away from thanksgiving and sets his eyes on proclaiming the gospel. He wants the gentiles to know he is in their debt so they can more easily hear the gospel story. Verses 14–16 might be a reminder to the gentiles that their new faith is a gift of the Jewish world and that they should accept the Jewish Christians returning from their expulsion with open hearts. Ultimately, Paul wants to communicate that the gentiles did not have to observe special practices or convert to Judaism in order to share this new faith. God is equally given to Jew and gentile alike. This is a theme Paul will return to again and again in this letter.

WORD STUDY NOTES #1

[1] Emperors in Rome, starting with Augustus, used the title "son of the gods" to describe themselves. As that practice grew in popularity, so did religious worship of the emperor, along with the erection of statues and temples to facilitate this worship and venerate the emperors. Whenever we see Paul or other New Testament writers using the phrase "Son of God" to refer to Jesus, they are making a familiar theological statement, but they are also making a provocative political statement in direct and intentional opposition to Rome.

3. Romans 1:18-20

In this section Paul really dives into the main part of his argument, and the gentile world is his focus. He wastes no time preparing them for the harsh words he speaks, immediately launching into a lecture about the wrath of God.[1] This might sound harsh to some today but for Paul, wrath and grace are two sides of the same coin. Paul does want to inform the gentiles of God's grace, but he also wants them to know there are consequences to flouting God as well—and he says they have no excuse.[2]

4. Romans 1:21–27

The latter half of Romans 1 is a contentious passage of Scripture today for obvious reasons. It touches on hot-button issues that generate strong feelings in many directions, but the main issue for Paul here is not the one many want to discuss.[1] Instead, he is focused on the disease of idolatry. The traits mentioned in the following verses are merely examples of symptoms of the disease.[2] Paul does not want the church in Rome merely to stop immoral behavior; he also wants them to worship God made flesh—the resurrected Christ. When humanity fails to worship God, we open ourselves to worship of that which is not worthy of our worship. The result of improper worship is clearly seen in Roman culture.[3]

5. Romans 1:28–32

Paul's description of God's wrath is that God simply let them have their way. The manner of God's judgment should be a sobering wake-up call for anyone who reads Romans 1. When God wants to release his wrath on people in rebellion, God simply lets us have our way. Even though Paul is specific about some sins, he is using them as examples of his larger point about idolatry.

WORD STUDY NOTES #3

[1] When we remove the worship of God from our lives, something else will take the place of God as lord of our lives. The wrath of God is often the natural result of who and what we follow.

[2] How were the gentiles supposed to know about Israel's God? Paul says God can be seen and known by all through the beauty and wonder of creation. The problem is that instead of worshiping the Creator, the world tends to worship the creation instead (like Roman emperors, for example).

WORD STUDY NOTES #4

[1] Paul does specifically mention certain sexual behaviors in Romans 1. This should not surprise us since Paul was Jewish. More than other religions of that day, Judaism held marriage in high regard. Sexual expression was meant to be celebrated between husband and wife in the home. That sexual ethic was to become the norm in the new church.

[2] Paul does not indicate in Romans 1 that homosexual practice triggers a special punishment. When Paul specifically mentions homosexual behavior, he is not lifting it above other sins but is using it as an example of how God's created order is being abandoned.

[3] Paul writes from Corinth. In the ancient world, temple worship of the gods was often a highly sexualized practice, especially in Corinth. When one failed to worship the one true God, the worship of many other gods led down a damaging sexual road.

Discoveries

Let's summarize our discoveries from Romans 1.

1. Calling Jesus the "Son of God" is an intentionally provocative and political act in first-century Rome.

2. God is equally given to the Jewish people and the gentiles. All have access through faith in Christ.

3. God has revealed who God is through the wonders of creation.

4. It is idolatry when we mistakenly worship what was created instead of the Creator.

5. According to Paul, God's wrath is not a violent or supernatural act of judgment from God but simply God letting humans experience the natural consequences of our own sin.

WEEK 1, DAY 4

Idolatry and the Story of God

Whenever we read a biblical text, it is important to ask how the text we are reading relates to the rest of the Bible. Romans 1 is not the only place in the Bible where people go their own way and suffer as a result of their decisions, nor is it the only place where the New Testament emphasizes the importance of Christ overcoming our divisions.

In the space provided below, write a short summary either of how idolatry impacts the lives of people or how faith in Christ should lead to unity among believers.

1. Genesis 11:1–9

_____

_____

_____

_____

_____

_____

_____

2. Exodus 32:1–30

_____

_____

_____

_____

_____

_____

_____

If you have a study Bible, it may have references in a margin, a middle column, or footnotes that point to other biblical texts. You may find it helpful in understanding how the whole story of God ties together to look up some of those other scriptures from time to time.

3. Jeremiah 7:12–29

_____

_____

_____

_____

_____

4. Daniel 3:1–18

_____

_____

_____

_____

_____

5. John 17:20–23

_____

_____

_____

_____

6. Ephesians 2:11–22

_____

_____

_____

_____

_____

7. Revelation 18:1–20

_____

_____

_____

_____

_____

WEEK 1, DAY 5

Romans and Our World Today

When we consider the themes of idolatry with its natural consequences and the human divisions we create as seen in Romans 1, we can see remarkable parallels to our own day and time. Romans 1 can become the lens through which we see ourselves, our world, and how God works in our world today.

1. Paul wishes peace to the church in Rome. How would a full understanding of peace impact believers today?

Peace is not an absence of conflict. But neither is peace the presence of violence. The church in Rome lived under the Pax Romana, which was the Roman Empire's way of achieving peace through violence, submission, and compliance. When Christians today seek peace, we should not be worried so much about everyone agreeing with everyone else but with treating people with the love that Christ has taught us. In Christ, our identities are secure, and our divisions disappear.

Following the above example, answer these questions about how we can understand ourselves, our world, and God's action in our world today.

2. Paul seems to specifically address groups that are typically overlooked. What people groups tend to be overlooked in our culture today?

_____

3. When Paul talks about "faith," what do you think he means?

_____

7

4. What can we know about God the Creator through observing creation?

_____

_____

_____

_____

_____

_____

_____

5. How do people worship created things rather than the Creator today, and how does it do damage?

_____

_____

_____

_____

_____

_____

_____

6. Paul has a big list of sinful behaviors here. Instead of reading the list and imagining others who commit these sins, which ones do you sometimes find present in yourself?

_____

_____

_____

_____

_____

_____

_____

_____

Invitation and Response

God's Word always invites a response. Think about the position of the church in Rome in relation to their larger culture, and think about the church today in relation to our larger culture. How does the text invite us to respond?

Paul's warning against idolatry is a relevant word for all ages. There is idolatry in the
Christian church today just as there was in the early church in Paul's day. Through Christ, we
have the power to reject idolatrous worship and refocus ourselves on our Creator.

What is your evaluation of yourself based on any or all of the verses found in Romans 1?

It is idolatry when we mistakenly worship what was created instead of the Creator.

ROMANS 2

After spending chapter 1 addressing the problems of the larger gentile world, Paul starts to turn his attention to his own people, the Jewish Christians. Paul has to convince the Jewish believers that the gentiles have full rights in the new church. Because the Jews have centuries of history as God's chosen people, Paul has a difficult task ahead of him. It will not be easy for the Jewish believers to see the gentiles as their equals. Paul's strategy is to emphasize faith over law, warning them that if their actions do not match their lofty words, their faith will not be respected, and in turn, Israel's God will never be honored.

The argument Paul makes to the Jewish believers sounds like it could have been written to the church today. Our world looks at our actions to see if our God is worthy of consideration and ultimately following.

WEEK 2, DAY 1

Absorb the passage in Romans 2 by reading it aloud several times until you become familiar with its verses, words, and phrases.

WEEK 2, DAY 2
ROMANS 2

The Setting

After their five-year expulsion from Rome, the Jews were allowed to return. Returning Jewish Christians found the budding church a different place than when they left. For years, Jews had been the foundation of the Christian church in Rome, and now they must have felt like strangers in their own church. Gentiles were different and, in the opinion of the Jewish Christians, had made too many allowances in the church. They would've happily received Paul's admonishments of the gentiles in Romans 1 and been eagerly awaiting more disciplinary words from Paul directed toward the gentiles as the letter continued.

The Message

In Romans 2, Paul turns his attention from the gentiles to his own people, the Jewish Christians. If the church were to forge a unified identity, they had to understand that sin was not a *gentile* condition but a *universal* one. This realization was born out of Paul's personal experience.

Paul had spent his entire life dedicated to Jewish law. He believed it was Israel's special responsibility to keep every command. His drive and zeal were so complete that he assumed great responsibility at a fairly young age, teaching correct doctrine to others and correcting wayward thinking in the synagogues. Paul was many things— but he was no hypocrite. On his way to enforce correct doctrine in Damascus, the unthinkable happened. His life was unexpectedly turned upside down when he encountered the risen Christ—which had nothing to do with the law. Paul had kept the law perfectly for his entire life, and it did not lead him closer to God at all. In fact, his zeal had pulled him somehow further away. The new reality for Paul was that knowledge of the law was not a guarantee of protection from sin.

To discover the message of Romans 2, let's divide the passage into five major sections. **Summarize or paraphrase the general message or theme of each section (following the pattern provided).**

1. Romans 2:1–4

2. Romans 2:5–11

3. Romans 2:12–16

4. Romans 2:17–24

Paul makes it clear he is addressing his fellow Jewish Christians in these verses.

What else do you see Paul saying here?

5. Romans 2:25–29

WEEK 2, DAY 3

What's Happening in the Passage?

As we read through these passages there are certain ideas and words that were familiar to the original readers but are not as familiar to us. Two thousand years and a vastly different culture obscure some of these ideas from us today. You may encounter some of these words and ideas in your study today. Some of them have been explained in more detail in the **Word Study Notes** below. If you want even more detail you can supplement this study with a Bible dictionary or commentary.

Create your own brief summary or description of the reality portrayed in verses 1–4.

WORD STUDY NOTES #1

[1] God's delay in judgment of sin is not God's tacit approval of sin. It is to give sinners a chance to repent. When we use God's patience as an opportunity to continue sin, we show disdain for God's mercy and grace. Such behavior is truly dangerous.

1. Romans 2:1-4[1]

_____

_____

_____

_____

_____

WORD STUDY NOTES #2

[1] Paul is telling the church that God does not favor one group over any other—which would've shocked the Jewish believers, since they've spent hundreds of years thinking God favored only them.

2. Romans 2:5-11

In this section Paul builds his case for a just and righteous God, who judges people according to the things they do, and the things they fail to do—"first for the Jew, then for the Gentile." Paul is saying that, just as God's message of hope was extended first to the Jew, so will God's justice and judgment also be for the Jews first.[1]

3. Romans 2:12–16

Paul tells the church that Jews and gentiles will be judged equally by God. A traditional Jew would find this impossible since the Jews had the inherent advantage of possessing the law. There is no way a gentile could satisfy the law since they were never given the law and did not know it. Therefore, the Jews had the advantage. Paul envisions a completely different standard: God will judge every person based on what they had the capacity to know, and their actions based on that knowledge. In Paul's new understanding the Jews who have the law will be judged according to the dictates of the law. The gentiles will be judged according to what they understand about God. This is why they are on equal footing.[1]

Create your own brief summary or description of the reality portrayed in verses 17–24.

4. Romans 2:17–24[1,2]

_____

_____

_____

_____

_____

5. Romans 2:25–29

To a people who have believed that the law was the central identifier of a Jew, Paul starts to change the definitions. Perhaps a Jew is not one who simply knows the law or possesses the law but one who *does* what the law requires. By subtly changing the expectation of what makes someone part of God's family, Paul has opened the door for widespread inclusion. A truly Jewish person, according to Paul, is one whose life exemplifies what the law always tried to create.[1] A gentile can respond even without the law, and a Jew by birth is not guaranteed to live rightly just because they recite the law in the synagogue. Both Jewish *and* gentile Christians[2] must choose to live differently.

WORD STUDY NOTES #3

[1] We are judged individually according to what we know, not according to what others know. The potential objection today might be: *How can I judge the actions of others if I do not know what other people know?* Paul's answer would be: *You can't, which is why judgment is better left to God.*

WORD STUDY NOTES #4

[1] There was a Jewish tendency to use the law as a shield. If they kept the demands of the law, then they were immune to sin. Paul's own experience convinced him that the law was not the defense he formerly believed it was.

[2] With his list of sins, Paul is not condemning every Jewish believer as guilty of every sin. He is trying to make the point that it does little good to claim to be the chosen people if one's actions stand in contrast to the claims made.

WORD STUDY NOTES #5

[1] Paul is using the word "Jew" as shorthand for a member of the family of God, since the central dividing issue between Jewish and gentile believers was whether gentiles could be considered God's people. Paul is expanding the boundaries.

[2] Paul did not think in terms of Jews "converting" to Christianity. The term "Jewish Christian" is a modern one used to distinguish the groups in the early church. Jewish followers of Jesus never saw themselves as anything *but* Jews. For Paul, being Jewish in the age of the resurrected Messiah was about following Christ and broadening the family of faith to include all who believed in Jesus.

Discoveries

Let's summarize our discoveries from Romans 2.

1. God's seeming slowness in judging sin is God's way of giving us every possible chance to repent.

2. God does not judge us according to standards we've never learned. God judges everyone fairly according to what they know.

3. When we (the children of God) live in hypocrisy—proclaiming what is right but not doing what is right—we make a mockery of God's name in the world.

4. Being part of the chosen family of God is not a birthright; it is an option for all, if we live by faith in Christ.

WEEK 2, DAY 4

Hypocrisy and the Story of God

Whenever we read a biblical text, it is important to ask how the text we are reading relates to the rest of the Bible. Romans 2 is not the only place in the Bible where people's actions fall short of their words. **In the space provided below, write a short summary of what each passage has to say about how hypocrisy ruins the witness of God's people.**

1. 2 Samuel 11:1–17

_____

_____

_____

_____

_____

_____

_____

2. Matthew 6:1–8

_____

_____

_____

_____

_____

_____

_____

_____

_____

If you have a study Bible, it may have references in a margin, a middle column, or footnotes that point to other biblical texts. You may find it helpful in understanding how the whole story of God ties together to look up some of those other scriptures from time to time.

3. Galatians 2:11–14

_____
_____
_____
_____
_____
_____
_____
_____
_____

4. 1 John 4:17–21

_____
_____
_____
_____
_____
_____
_____
_____
_____
_____

5. James 2:14–26

_____
_____
_____
_____
_____
_____
_____
_____
_____
_____

WEEK 2, DAY 5

Romans and Our World Today

When we consider the issues that faced the church in Rome, Romans 2 can become the lens through which we see ourselves, our world, and how God works in our world today.

1. Why is favoritism a dangerous practice in any church?

We are often tempted to think that "we" have advantages over "them." It threatens the witness
and the unity of the church if we let this worldly temptation infect our thinking as Christians.
Paul was very concerned about either major group in the Roman church-Jewish believers or
gentiles-thinking they were better than the other.

Following the above example, answer these questions about how we can understand ourselves, our world, and God's action in our world today.

2. What activities do modern Christians do that tend to replace vital faith?

3. How do our own words and actions not match today? (Note the wording *our own*. This is not a question about other people's words and actions.)

4. How do Paul's words in Romans 2 impact your understanding of what happens to those who never have the opportunity to hear the gospel?

_____

_____

_____

_____

_____

_____

_____

_____

_____

_____

_____

5. Does the thought of being judged based on what we have the chance to know comfort us or unsettle us?

_____

_____

_____

_____

_____

_____

_____

_____

_____

_____

_____

_____

_____

Invitation and Response

God's Word always invites a response. Think about the way the themes of equality and/or hypocrisy speak to us today. How does Romans 2 invite us to respond?

There are times when Christians seem to think pretty highly of ourselves, especially for those in the Holiness tradition. We must always remember that a wider world is watching our actions and comparing them to our words. If our actions fall short of our claims, then the faith we espouse and the God we proclaim falls into disrepute. This is never more true than when we seem to be unaware of the gap. When we consider a list of the most damaging sins in the eyes of the world, hypocrisy by Christians might be at the top of that list.

What is your evaluation of yourself based on any or all of the verses found in Romans 2?

God's seeming slowness in judging
sin is God's way of giving us every
possible chance to repent.

44

ROMANS 3

The first two chapters of Romans reflect not only the situation of the church in Rome but also a wider issue in all the New Testament churches. There is a divide, and often a distrust, between the Jewish believers and their gentile counterparts. Since an ongoing division would be catastrophic for this important church, Paul speaks to the larger gentile culture first, then to the returning Jews. In both instances Paul's argument is that both groups are willing perpetrators of sin and therefore both stand guilty. There is no room in the new church for one group lording special status over another.

The potential consequences of Paul's words are immense. The gentile believers could accuse Paul of hating Rome or of being prejudiced against non-Jewish believers. The Jewish Christians could accuse Paul of betraying the faith and appeasing gentiles.

Before he could move forward with a unified church, Paul would need to explain what the two groups have in common, which is where chapter 3 comes in.

WEEK 3, DAY 1

Absorb the passage in Romans 3 by reading it aloud several times until you become familiar with its verses, words, and phrases.

The Setting

After the first two chapters, Paul has carefully and methodically demonstrated a new and necessary position to the church in Rome: Jews and gentiles stand on equal footing before God. Gentiles would not be surprised by this statement, but the Jews would have found it shocking. After centuries of perceiving themselves to be God's chosen people with a divine purpose, hearing that God does not show them favoritism would be a surprise. Even as Paul makes this argument, he anticipates the logical question Jewish believers would inevitably ask: *If our status as chosen people does not grant us an inside track to God, then what good does the law even serve?*

The Message

While this seems like a legitimate question, Paul does not intend to communicate that the Jewish people no longer have a unique role. Paul does not think the law is useless, but he emphasizes that its importance is different than what the Jewish believers think. Not only is the law still important, but it is also vital for the gentiles. Paul now explains why both Jews and gentiles are important and how the law informs all of humanity.

In chapter 3, Paul speaks to a new, unified church—not only to gentiles or only to Jews specifically. By the end of this chapter, we will see not only that all of humanity shares the same problem but also the remedy God provides and the unique role the law can play in that remedy.

To discover the message of Romans 3, let's divide the passage into six sections. **Summarize or paraphrase the general message or theme of each section.**

47

1. Romans 3:1–4

_____

_____

_____

_____

_____

_____

_____

_____

2. Romans 3:5–8

_____

_____

_____

_____

_____

_____

_____

_____

_____

3. Romans 3:9–18

_____

_____

_____

_____

_____

_____

_____

_____

_____

4. Romans 3:19–20

5. Romans 3:21–26

6. Romans 3:27–31

What's Happening in the Passage?

As we read through these passages there are certain ideas and words that were familiar to the original readers but are not as familiar to us. Two thousand years and a vastly different culture obscure some of these ideas from us today. You may encounter some of these words and ideas in your study today. Some of them have been explained in more detail in the **Word Study Notes** below. If you want even more detail you can supplement this study with a Bible dictionary or commentary.

WORD STUDY NOTES #1

[1] Paul wants to affirm that, just because the role for the Jews is not what they think, that does not mean there is no special relationship between them and God.

50

1. Romans 3:1-4

Paul begins chapter 3 with an anticipated objection to what he has stated so far. If God does not show favoritism (2:11), then is there anything sacred or special about being Jewish? Paul's answer is definitively positive. Yes, Judaism is unique.[1] Another potential objection would be to question the relationship God had with the Jews since the Jews were not faithful as God's people. Paul once again answers in the strongest language when asked if God's faithfulness is nullified by Israel's infidelity: "Not at all!" Paul argues that, even if Israel is unfaithful, God's faithfulness to the covenant remains.

2. Romans 3:5-8

There is one other objection that Paul anticipates he must adequately answer. Paul has already stated that the Jews are guilty of sin even though they possess the law. Now he has argued there is still something special about the Jewish believers. The logical question Paul anticipated was, if the Jews were sinful but the law still has value, then why worry about sin? Since our failure showcases God's holiness, then maybe we should just keep sinning. Paul forcefully objects to this line of reasoning.

3. Romans 3:9–18

After hearing Paul's words about the law, some might once again conclude that the Jews have a special path to God that others do not have. Paul repeats his earlier argument and says no. Jews and gentiles are equally impacted by the presence and power of sin. At this point, Paul quotes extensively from a number of different Psalms, and one verse from Isaiah, to emphasize the tendency of people to sin.

Create your own brief summary or description of the reality portrayed in verses 19–20.

4. Romans 3:19–20[1, 2]

_____

_____

_____

_____

_____

_____

_____

_____

_____

_____

_____

_____

_____

_____

_____

_____

_____

_____

WORD STUDY NOTES #4

[1] The phrase "works of the law" is often understood today to mean "good deeds." But Paul is referring to the "works" that Jewish people performed in order to mark themselves _in the eyes of others_ as God's chosen people—things like circumcision, food laws, observance of the Sabbath and other holy days. Paul is saying that Jewish Christians were perverting these markers to claim special status over the gentiles, relying on their ethnic identity for their salvation rather than on faith in Jesus.

[2] Jews might've felt despair at Paul's declaration about nobody being declared righteous through the law. If they could not be declared righteous through the sacred law, then they might have wondered what hope there was for them.

[1] Our understanding of Paul's use of righteousness comes straight from the Old Testament in connection with the covenant. The righteous uphold the covenant and preserve the covenant relationship. The unrighteous are not faithful to the covenant and therefore destroy the relationship by their actions. When God is described as righteous, God is being faithful to the covenant. When we are described as righteous, we are placed within the covenant community, even if we are gentiles.

[2] Paul describes the sacrifice of Jesus in a way the Jewish believers would understand. Every year, the Jewish high priest offered a perfect lamb for a sacrifice of atonement. Paul is helping them understand that Jesus takes the place of the sacrificial lamb.

5. Romans 3:21-26

Paul's focus shifts to the solution for our predicament, stating there is a righteousness that comes from God by simple faith. This faith is not a new development but was described by both the law and the Old Testament prophets. Paul is telling the believers that righteousness[1] was God's plan from the beginning and that the law was given to serve this faith. Our faith does not serve the law. Gentiles and Jews alike share equally in both the sin *and* the grace offered by God. Paul explains that Jesus is our sacrifice.[2] Because he tasted death, we no longer need to.

6. Romans 3:27–31

Paul shows his line of reasoning in the whole of chapter 3 when he talks about boasting. If they could be righteous by observing the law—in other words, by proving what good Jews they were—then they could feel proud. Paul is scolding the Jewish believers for letting this happen because, in their attentiveness to the law, they separated themselves from others, viewed themselves as superior, and failed to be the light for the gentiles that God wanted them to be. Further, Paul says, if observing the law was the path to righteousness, then only Jews could become righteous and God would only be God *for* the Jews (and gentiles who fully converted to Judaism). Paul explicitly states that there is only one God for both Jews and gentiles. There seems to be no room for the law in Paul's argument, but Paul says all of this means the law is upheld. Yet the explanation for how or why is left for later chapters.

Discoveries

Let's summarize our discoveries from Romans 3.

1. The chosen-ness and special status of the Jewish people was always meant to bring the rest of the world (i.e., the gentiles) into the family of God.

2. God's faithfulness cannot be nullified by our unfaithfulness.

3. A common trait of humanity is that, although we like to divide ourselves by various boundary lines, we are united in that we all tend to gravitate toward sinful behavior.

4. There is nothing we can do to set ourselves apart as more special than anyone else in God's creation.

5. Just as all humans sin, so are all humans eligible for the salvation God desires to offer us.

Equality and the Story of God

Whenever we read a biblical text, it is important to ask how the text we are reading relates to the rest of the Bible. Romans 3 is not the only place where the divide between Jewish and gentile believers is addressed. **In the space provided below, write a short summary of what each passage has to say about the Jewish-gentile divide.**

1. Acts 15:5–11

_____

_____

_____

_____

2. Galatians 2:6–10

_____

_____

_____

_____

3. Ephesians 1:3–14

_____

_____

_____

_____

4. Colossians 2:16–23

_____

_____

_____

_____

If you have a study Bible, it may have references in a margin, a middle column, or footnotes that point to other biblical texts. You may find it helpful in understanding how the whole story of God ties together to look up some of those other scriptures from time to time.

WEEK 3, DAY 5

Romans and Our World Today

When we consider the issues that faced the church in Rome, Romans 3 can become the lens through which we see ourselves, our world, and how God works in our world today.

1. Paul anticipated the question that, if our sinfulness showcases God's holiness, then doesn't that mean it's fine if we keep sinning? How would Paul respond to this logic in our world today?

Some have said that, since going to church does not make one automatically a Christian, then why worry about going to church or raising children in the faith? Paul's answer would be that there is value in hearing the gospel. It is vital to have people who can tell the world about what God has done and is doing. Just like the Jews had the responsibility to show God to the world and expand the family of God by using their special status to include others, so do Christians today have that same responsibility. This obligation given to the people of God is an honor that should never be forgotten or taken for granted.

Following the above example, answer these questions about how we can understand ourselves, our world, and God's action in our world today.

2. What special considerations do you think people who have been Christians a long time feel over people who are new Christians (similar to how the Jewish believers felt superior to the gentiles)?

3. How do we determine which guidelines, or boundaries, are necessary today and which ones might be unnecessary obstacles?

_____

_____

_____

_____

_____

_____

4. What dangers are there when the church treats non-essential beliefs or practices as essential?

_____

_____

_____

_____

_____

5. What kind of damage is done to the church and its witness when divisions remain within the church?

_____

_____

_____

_____

_____

_____

_____

_____

Invitation and Response

God's Word always invites a response. Think about the way the themes of unity and equality speak to us today. How does Romans 3 invite us to respond?

_____

_____

_____

_____

_____

_____

_____

_____

_____

_____

_____

What is your evaluation of yourself based on any or all of the verses found in Romans 3?

_____

_____

_____

_____

_____

_____

_____

_____

_____

_____

_____

_____

_____

_____

God's faithfulness
cannot be nullified by
our unfaithfulness.

ROMANS 4

Paul has just ended chapter 3 by claiming that gentiles and Jews are on equal footing before God; both have access to God by faith. In chapter 4 Paul wants to use an example of this faith from the beloved Hebrew scriptures — something that shows how the standard can be applied to Jew and gentile alike. Paul finds his example in Abraham, the person the Jews consider their forefather. To make his case, Paul must present Abraham as a man of faith who became the head of the covenant family by faith alone.

WEEK 4, DAY 1

Absorb the passage in Romans 4 by reading it aloud several times until you become familiar with its verses, words, and phrases.

WEEK 4, DAY 2

The Setting

Paul has used the first three chapters of Romans to argue for a central point of his theology: Jews and gentiles are equally part of the church. Paul demonstrated the sinful condition of both groups Thankfully, he also declared that both groups can equally access the redemption offered through Christ. Because this concept is going to be radical for his Jewish audience, Paul feels the need to support his claims using Jewish scriptures (what we often call the Old Testament today) as proof that this idea is neither new nor outside of Jewish tradition.

The Message

Paul often uses Abraham to illustrate his points. Abraham was the patriarch of patriarchs for the Jews. He was the first to respond to Israel's God. In some Hebrew traditions, Abraham condemned the building of the tower of Babel. Abraham journeyed to the mountain with his son Isaac and heard the voice of God direct him personally. Abraham stood at the pinnacle of Israel's history. If something was true for Abraham, it was good for the Jewish people.

Another reason Paul liked to use Abraham as an example is that God established the covenant relationship with Abraham hundreds of years before the law was given at Sinai. Whatever God did through Abraham was of particular interest to Paul since Paul, like Abraham, was attempting to create a new people not based on the presence of the law.

To discover the message of Romans 4, let's divide the passage into four sections. **Summarize or paraphrase the general message or theme of each section.**

1. Romans 4:1–8

_____

_____

_____

_____

_____

_____

2. Romans 4:9–12

3. Romans 4:13–17

4. Romans 4:18–25

WEEK 4, DAY 3

What's Happening in the Passage?

As we read through these passages there are certain ideas and words that were familiar to the original readers but are not as familiar to us. Two thousand years and a vastly different culture obscure some of these ideas from us today. You may encounter some of these words and ideas in your study today. Some of them have been explained in more detail in the **Word Study Notes** below. If you want even more detail you can supplement this study with a Bible dictionary or commentary.

1. Romans 4:1–8

In this chapter Paul presents the life of Abraham as the example for the young church to follow. Abraham is nothing less than the prototypical Jew—yet he is only part of God's family by faith. God promised to bless Abraham and, through Abraham, to bless all nations. When God told Abraham to go to a new land, Abraham went, and when God told him his descendants would be as numerous as the stars, Abraham believed. For Paul, Abraham's actions represent the same type of faith that the believers in his day were to have in Christ. Paul's argument is relatively straightforward. If grace comes through human effort, then it is no longer a gift but an obligation owed to the one who worked for it. There is nothing we can do that contributes to our redemption because it is dependent on the death and resurrection of Christ. We freely receive the gift of God that we did not deserve in any way. This the crux of the matter for Paul.

2. Romans 4:9–12

Often, the Jewish-gentile issue fell along lines defined by Genesis 15 and 17. When Paul entered a new location, he preached from Genesis 15: "Abraham believed God, and it was credited to him as righteousness." Opponents who followed Paul presented a message from Genesis 17:10: "Every male among you must be circumcised."[1] That is why Paul's reference to circumcision follows on the heels of his discussion of Abraham. Jewish

WORD STUDY NOTES #2

[1] Practices like circumcision and following food laws made the Jewish people distinct in the world. They did these things to be faithful to Judaism and thus—in their thinking—to *keep* their status, not to earn it.

[2] This means that Abraham is the father of the Jews as well as anyone who comes to Christ through faith.

believers know that Abraham was considered righteous by God well before he was ever circumcised. Therefore, Abraham is the father of the Jews not because of circumcision but because of his simple faith.[2]

Create your own brief summary or description of the reality portrayed in verses 13–17.

3. Romans 4:13–17[1, 2]

WORD STUDY NOTES #3

[1] Paul uses the word "offspring" first to describe the Jews (v. 13), and then to refer to all who come to Christ through faith (v. 16).

[2] There is a larger issue behind Paul's insistence that Jews and gentiles alike are Abraham's offspring. Deuteronomy 6:4 proclaims one God instead of many (monotheism over polytheism). Paul's argument is that, if only Jews can be part of God's family, then there must be another God for the gentiles. Paul is certain there isn't; therefore, God is God of all.

_____

_____

_____

_____

_____

_____

_____

_____

4. Romans 4:18–25

There was no reason for Abraham to believe he would father a child at his advanced age, and even less reason to believe Sarah could give birth at that age. God would have to do the impossible. The point Paul is making is not about active belief on Abraham's part but the realization that God would have to step in. It wasn't believable, so there was only hope. In fact, Abraham's actions betrayed hope. He tried to get himself the promised son by means other than Sarah (remember Hagar and Ishmael?). Paul is saying Abraham's faith came at the point "against all hope" — when he realized he could not produce the promise of God through his own effort. Centuries of Jewish striving with the law never produced the righteousness they desired. Now gentiles are coming to God through Christ and no striving of their own. It all depends on God. Abraham ultimately had to believe in a God who gives life to the dead, and Christians believe in a God who raised Jesus from the dead. This is our hope.

Discoveries

Let's summarize our discoveries from Romans 4.

1. Abraham—the quintessential example of what it means to be a Jew, and the father of all Jews—was brought into the family of God by faith, not by the law.

2. God's blessing of Abraham because Abraham believed and obeyed—not because Abraham was circumcised, which only came *after* he believed—indicates that God always intended to include gentiles in the family of faith.

3. Abraham therefore becomes the father of all God's people—Jewish and gentile—because of faith, not because of the law.

4. Hope can only come once we understand that our human efforts are futile; only then can we have the capacity to hope for God's action.

If you have a study Bible, it may have references in a margin, a middle column, or footnotes that point to other biblical texts. You may find it helpful in understanding how the whole story of God ties together to look up some of those other scriptures from time to time.

Faith, Hope, and the Story of God

Whenever we read a biblical text, it is important to ask how the text we are reading relates to the rest of the Bible. Romans 4 is not the only place where God's blessing for those who have faith, regardless of their background, is apparent. **In the space provided below, write a short summary of what each passage has to say about the role of faith or hope in the life of a person who follows God.**

1. Genesis 12:1–5

_____

_____

_____

_____

_____

_____

_____

2. Judges 6:12–40

_____

_____

_____

_____

_____

_____

_____

_____

3. 1 Kings 19:9–19

_____

_____

_____

_____

_____

_____

_____

_____

_____

4. Luke 8:40–48

_____

_____

_____

_____

_____

_____

_____

_____

_____

5. Acts 16:6–15

_____

_____

_____

_____

_____

_____

_____

_____

_____

WEEK 4, DAY 5

Romans and Our World Today

When we consider the issues that faced the church in Rome, Romans 4 can become the lens through which we see ourselves, our world, and how God works in our world today.

1. How do modern Christians think they are scoring points with God by either doing certain things or avoiding other things?

Sometimes we get caught up in our ideas of what we should be doing or should not be doing if
we are God's people, and instead of focusing on the love of Christ, we focus instead on actions.
When we focus too much on actions, we often can lose the ties these actions have to Christ,
and we end up following rules for the sake of rules rather than because they bring us closer to
Christ. Similarly, this attitude can also make us unfairly judgmental of others who don't
perform the same actions in the same way we do. Paul would have something to say about that!

Following the above example, answer these questions about how we can understand ourselves, our world, and God's action in our world today.

2. How do we complicate the idea of coming to Christ through simple faith? What do we add?

_____

_____

_____

_____

_____

_____

_____

_____

_____

_____

_____

3. What groups of people today do Christians exclude from being part of God's people, or what conditions do Christians put on people before allowing them to be included? How does this make us more like the Jewish Christians Paul is addressing in Romans than we realize?

_____

_____

_____

_____

_____

_____

4. How can Abraham be a model for us today? How did he falter, and where was he faithful?

_____

_____

_____

_____

_____

_____

_____

5. How can focusing on Jesus, rather than our actions, give us more confidence in our faith?

_____

_____

_____

_____

_____

_____

_____

_____

Invitation and Response

God's Word always invites a response. Think about the way the themes of simple faith and impossible hope speak to us today. How does Romans invite us to respond?

Paul above all wants the believers in Rome to understand that Abraham was not chosen by God for his good actions or his faithful living. Abraham was a nobody who had done nothing to earn God's grace! How can that be an example for us today?

_____

_____

_____

_____

_____

_____

_____

What is your evaluation of yourself based on any or all of the verses found in Romans 4?

_____

_____

_____

_____

_____

_____

_____

_____

_____

_____

_____

_____

_____

_____

_____

_____

God always intended
to include gentiles in
the family of faith.

ROMANS 5

Paul has just demonstrated that faithfulness has always been the standard for God's people, using Abraham as his model. It is an effective argument since Abraham was seen as someone who was faithful even before the law was given. His faithfulness was best demonstrated in the near sacrifice of Isaac, an event that was critically important to the Jewish people. At key points in his life, Abraham trusted God completely; as a result, God made him the father of the Jews.

At the end of chapter 4, Paul draws a parallel between the faith of Abraham and the faith of anyone who believes Jesus rose from the dead. That simple faith changes the life of every believer. A new believer might ask: *how does simple faith make such a difference?* In Romans 5, Paul answers that question for the individual and for all of humanity.

WEEK 5, DAY 1

Absorb the passage in Romans 5 by reading it aloud several times until you become familiar with its verses, words, and phrases.

WEEK 5, DAY 2

The Setting

Having made the case for simple faith instead of observing the law as the catalyst for a relationship with God, Paul spells out the consequences of this standard. First, Paul talks about what it means in the lives of individual believers. The first benefit is that we have peace and hope in God. The totalitarian specter of Rome should not be forgotten at this point. Life was difficult in the first century, and there was an extreme power imbalance between the average believer and the immense power of Rome. It would be easy to succumb to hopelessness. Paul would say we have hope not because there is a guaranteed outcome but because there is a guaranteed presence, even in the midst of hardship and persecution.

The Message

In this part of the letter Paul explains in detail the problem of sin, the impact of the law, and God's answer to the problem of sin and death. To discover the message of Romans 5, let's examine the passage by dividing it into four sections. **Summarize or paraphrase the general message or theme of each section.**

1. Romans 5:1–5

_____

_____

_____

_____

_____

2. Romans 5:6–11

_____

_____

_____

_____

_____

3. Romans 5:12–14

4. Romans 5:15–21

WEEK 5, DAY 3

What's Happening in the Passage?

As we read through these passages there are certain ideas and words that were familiar to the original readers but are not as familiar to us. Two thousand years and a vastly different culture obscure some of these ideas from us today. You may encounter some of these words and ideas in your study today. Some of them have been explained in more detail in the **Word Study Notes** below. If you want even more detail you can supplement this study with a Bible dictionary or commentary.

Create your own brief description of Paul's words in 5:1–5.

1. Romans 5:1–5[1, 2]

_____

_____

_____

_____

_____

_____

2. Romans 5:6–11

Paul says we can be confident that God loves us because, when we were powerless and could offer nothing in return, Christ walked in our midst and ultimately died for us. This depth of love and sacrificial death is how God demonstrates his grace to us. When we were at our worst Christ showed his best by dying for us when we had nothing to offer. [1] Now that believers have been justified, our relationship to God can be restored, something that is accomplished through the death and resurrection of Jesus.

WORD STUDY NOTES #1

[1] Whenever we see the word "therefore" in the Bible, we know that means the writer is referencing something that was previously said. So it's important to look at how chapter 4 ends in order to gain full context for what Paul is talking about here in the beginning of chapter 5.

[2] Paul wants to contrast new life in Christ with those who build their lives around observing the law. Though he doesn't mention the law here, he is acknowledging it by implication: some boast in their possession of the law, but we boast only in what Christ accomplished on our behalf.

WORD STUDY NOTES #2

[1] The New Testament world operated within a cultural system where people typically only did nice things for those whom they knew could return the favor, and when favors were done for people, the expectation was that they would be reciprocated. Jesus turned that entire system upside down.

3. Romans 5:12–14

This is the part of Romans where Paul begins to examine the sin problem of humanity in depth. Paul says that the proof we have of sin in the world is the overwhelming existence of death, reminding his readers of Adam and Eve's sin in Genesis. In verses 12 through the early part of verse 14, Paul uses the common word *hamartia* for sin.[1] Some wonder when we become accountable for the sin we commit. All of us live less than flawlessly. Paul's words enrich our understanding. His standard is that we must be *aware* of the wrong that we do in order to be guilty. In verse 14 Paul has the Ten Commandments clearly in mind as he tells the readers that sin was active well before the law was given. Paul uses a different word for Adam's sin. It was not *hamartia* but *parabasis*—purposeful rebellion.[2] He knew what should not be done and did it anyway. Rebellion has consequences.

4. Romans 5:15–19

Paul compares Adam to Christ. Adam's sin—which changed the trajectory of humanity—was purposeful. The action Christ took to reverse the damage was also deliberate. For Paul, sin was comprehensive, and its presence damaged every area of life. The effects of sin permeate every level of reality—which is why the sacrifice of Christ was a fitting response. When sin seeks to destroy, it finds an even more powerful grace. The pervasiveness of evil is confronted and defeated by an even more powerful grace. This is the good news of the gospel.

5. Romans 5:20–21

Verse 20 undoubtedly confused early Jewish believers in the Roman church, just as it confuses us today. When Paul states that the law was given so that "the trespass might increase," it sounds like he is denigrating the law. Instead, this verse explains what Paul earlier stated Romans 3:20: "through the law we become conscious of sin." Paul has already admitted earlier in this chapter that sin is evident in the world. Sin is simply all around us, and it rules the world. However, sin is not held against us without the presence of the law. Here at the end of chapter 5, Paul is explaining how the law is used to charge sin to our account. In order for grace to overcome sin, we must become aware that sin is something for which we are responsible. The law does have a vital role, but it is not the role formerly thought. It does not bring life or make someone good. The law tells us we are not good and that we are in need of redemption. Paul assured the believers that grace is greater than sin because, if we never know we are in need, then our lack of knowledge actually keeps us from experiencing the new life that Christ brings. For the sick, a diagnosis is necessary for healing; so it is with sin.

WORD STUDY NOTES #3

[1] *Hamartia* is by far the word used most in the New Testament for sin. *Hamartia* means anything that misses the mark, or the intended aim. What we are aiming at is just as important as whether we hit our mark. *Hamartia* does not refer only to individual lives but also collective society. Death, sin, and pain—and the consequences that those things bring to the world—are not what God intended for the world.

[2] There are a number of synonyms for sin that Paul uses in chapter 5—and not interchangeably. *Hamartia*: any action that misses the intended mark. *Paraptoma*: a deliberate stepping across a line; purposeful and intentional. *Parabasis*: rebellion. We live in a world dominated by *hamartia* and death is the proof, but Paul is adamant that willful sin is what is charged against us.

Discoveries

Let's summarize our discoveries from Romans 5.

1. Christ's incarnation, death, and resurrection on our behalf are definitive proof that God loves us.

2. There are different kinds of sin in the world—sin that misses the mark, intentional sin, individual sin, collective/social sin. We are held accountable for when we intentionally rebel or cross the line.

3. Sin has long-lasting and far-reaching effects in every part of the world, most notably death—which is why we boast in Christ's accomplishment over death on our behalf.

4. The power of sin is not as powerful as the grace of God.

WEEK 5, DAY 4

Sin and the Story of God

Whenever we read a biblical text, it is important to ask how the text we are reading relates to the rest of the Bible. Romans 5 is not the only place in the Bible where we are reminded about the presence of sin in our lives. **In the space provided below, write a short summary of how our experience with sin is navigated in these other passages.**

1. Genesis 3:14–24

_____

_____

_____

_____

_____

2. Genesis 11:1–9

_____

_____

_____

_____

_____

3. Psalm 51:1–12

_____

_____

_____

_____

_____

If you have a study Bible, it may have references in a margin, a middle column, or footnotes that point to other biblical texts. You may find it helpful in understanding how the whole story of God ties together to look up some of those other scriptures from time to time.

4. Jeremiah 31:27–30

5. Luke 18:18–25

WEEK 5, DAY 5

Romans and Our World Today

When we consider the issue of sin in Scripture and in our world, Romans 5 can become the lens through which we see ourselves, our world, and how God works in our world today.

1. Paul talks a lot about our relationship with God being restored, or reconciled. What does this mean for us today?

One of the key words in Romans is "righteousness." For Paul, righteousness is the state that is opposite our natural state of sin. It is a free gift that flows from Christ to the believer (see Romans 5:17). This free gift is accessed through simple faith, as evidenced by Abraham (see Romans 4:5). The righteous life is characterized by obedience to God, which is a product of an active relationship with God, not adherence to Jewish regulations.

Following the above example, answer these questions about how we can understand ourselves, our world, and God's action in our world today.

2. What are some examples of how sin reigns in our world?

3. How do you think the power of sin is transferred from generation to generation?

4. What are the various ways we come to a knowledge of right and wrong, or of what God expects from us?

_____

_____

_____

_____

_____

_____

_____

_____

5. In your life, what might be an example of missing the mark as opposed to intentional rebellion or stepping over the line?

_____

_____

_____

_____

_____

_____

_____

_____

6. How can knowledge of a higher standard create the desire for sin?

_____

_____

_____

_____

_____

_____

_____

_____

Invitation and Response

God's Word always invites a response. Think about the way the themes of sin and righteousness (or reconciliation) speak to us today. How do they invite us to respond?

_____

_____

_____

_____

_____

_____

_____

_____

_____

What is your evaluation of yourself based on any or all of the verses found in Romans 5?

_____

_____

_____

_____

_____

_____

_____

_____

_____

_____

_____

> The power of sin is not as
> powerful as the grace of God.

ROMANS 6

The early chapters of Romans describe the way Jews and gentiles alike are under the power of sin. In chapter 5, Paul's description of sin turns personal: it is important to realize that everyone sins, but it is vital to remember that sin is an individual problem as well as a collective one. The law only reveals our sin; it does not solve the problem. Thankfully, Paul says, there is a power even greater than sin, and that power is grace. Because of what Christ has done, we have a choice about which power we will serve.

WEEK 6, DAY 1

Absorb the passage in Romans 6 by reading it aloud several times until you become familiar with its verses, words, and phrases.

WEEK 6, DAY 2

The Setting

The problem of sin is still at the center of this section of Romans. Paul has already declared that the Jews do not have an inside track to God and that their careful observance of the law does not bring them closer to God. At the end of chapter 5, Paul intensified his argument and told the believers that the law actually serves to increase sin. Sin is more than a general sense of wrongdoing; because of the law, it is willfully going against God. If this is the case, what help is there for humanity? How does Christ free us from the power of sin?

The Message

Paul has set the stage by telling his readers that sin and grace stand in opposition to each other. The good news for the believers is that grace is more powerful than sin. As a result, where the law comes in and identifies sin, it does so in order that grace might overcome sin. Because of Christ, anyone who calls on Jesus cannot continue to sin. Grace forgives our sin, compels us to walk free from sin, and empowers the believer to triumph over sin in the future. Romans 6 describes how grace works in the life of the believer.

The early believers may have been filled with many of the questions that we still ask today: *How does Christ live within us? After accepting Jesus, do we lose our free will? Are we under the control of a greater power?* Somehow, life in Christ transforms our lives in new and surprising ways. We find the same transforming power at work in other relationships as well. Paul wants his readers to know that relationships require love. At the heart of grace is love that was poured out for us from the cross. This grace always demands a response.

To discover the message of Romans 6, let's examine the passage by dividing it into five sections. **Summarize or paraphrase the general message or theme of each section.**

1. Romans 6:1–4

---

2. Romans 6:5–10

_____

_____

_____

_____

_____

_____

3. Romans 6:11–14

_____

_____

_____

_____

_____

_____

4. Romans 6:15–18

_____

_____

_____

_____

_____

_____

5. Romans 6:19–23

_____

_____

_____

_____

_____

_____

WEEK 6, DAY 3

What's Happening in the Passage?

As we read through these passages there are certain ideas and words that were familiar to the original readers but are not as familiar to us. Two thousand years and a vastly different culture obscure some of these ideas from us today. You may encounter some of these words and ideas in your study today. Some of them have been explained in more detail in the **Word Study Notes** below. If you want even more detail you can supplement this study with a Bible dictionary or commentary.

1. Romans 6:1–4

Chapter 6 opens with a strong question. If grace abounds all the more, should we then keep on sinning? Paul's answer is abundantly clear and is again expressed in the strongest language available to him: "by no means!" Something has happened that forever changes how we live. We have died to sin and are raised with Christ.[1] Our past does not determine our present or future in Christ. Paul strongly links this distinct moment with baptism, which is a change in life marked by a change of lords—no longer a subject of Caesar but now belonging to Christ. Baptism is a change of lords from Caesar to Christ—and also from Adam to Christ. The symbolic power of baptism is a statement that we no longer want to be dominated by the effects of Adam's sin but instead desire to participate in the benefits of Christ's resurrection.

2. Romans 6:5–10

Paul also makes it clear that we are not experiencing a solitary spiritual event but are being integrated into something much greater. We are now united with Christ's body. This imagery is meant to demonstrate that the event that brings us life was a real, physical event for Christ. It is also a reminder that we are now part of a body of Christ that exists in a local church but also with everyone around the world who finds their identity in Christ. In the first century, Paul had to battle the prevalent Gnosticism of the age, reiterating that even though we cannot escape our bodies, we *can* escape sin's control.[1] Paul said we are also united with Christ in his resurrection—able to enjoy new

WORD STUDY NOTES #1

[1] Some have made the mistake of thinking that "died to sin" means that the capacity for sin, or our inclination to sin, ends with initial belief. The intent of this verse is to remind the believer that the former self is dead, along with the way of life that accompanied our former self. The verb translated as "died" is in a Greek tense that indicates a completed moment with ongoing consequences. While it points to the past, we live in the active results of that decisive moment.

WORD STUDY NOTES #2

[1] Gnosticism is the dualistic belief that the physical world is corrupt and evil while the spiritual world is pure. Some believed it was okay for the body to experience a host of sins because it could not touch the soul. Paul strongly denounces this belief.

[1] There is an important distinction to acknowledge between the lie that we are *unable* to sin and the truth Paul is proclaiming that we have the ability *not* to sin. This ability springs from the grace of God and the power of the Holy Spirit.

[2] This language implies choice. We have the ability to choose who or what our master will be. It is a given for Paul that believers would have no desire to choose sin.

WORD STUDY NOTES #4

[1] This term suggests more than just the legal consideration of justification. We can live with a certain distance from the pervasive power of sin.

WORD STUDY NOTES #5

[1] Paul wants his audience to remember that we have a choice. We either intentionally offer ourselves to God, or we choose to become part of ever-increasing sin. There are only two choices with starkly different consequences.

[2] The Roman system of slavery was vastly different from the chattel system practiced in the U.S. and the British Empire. In ancient Rome, slavery could be entered voluntarily, and could be fairly lucrative. Plato, for instance, was a slave. However, slaves were bound to their master, who could control their lives. Voluntary participation in slavery is the background for this entire section. Paul is saying that followers of Christ have the power to choose the one to whom they will grant control.

[3] Holiness is far more than the absence of sin. Believers may be considered holy in the sense that they are in relationship to God. When we live in active relationship with God, we will be different. Holiness is being filled with God. It is a life of completeness, well-being, restored relationships, and moral sensibilities. It is not done in isolation but in the midst of our broken world. We live not for ourselves but for Christ and for the benefit of the world around us.

life now, and have freedom from sin and a new relationship with God, while also awaiting final resurrection.

3. Romans 6:11–14

If we have died to sin and been raised with Christ, therefore we are not to let sin reign or succumb to its temptations. This command is not an automatic condition but a hopeful possibility. Sin is still active as a force in the world, but if we are dead to its call, we can and should live differently.[1] Treating our faith as a one-time decision will not help us defeat the power of sin in our lives. Instead, Paul says we must "offer ourselves to God."[2] We must have an active and ongoing relationship with God in Christ, whose presence alone is what enables us to live without succumbing to sin.

4. Romans 6:15–18

Paul continues to starkly present sin and obedience in opposition to each other. Any argument that sin is not worrisome because grace will cover it is anathema to Paul. Even a solitary sin places the believer on a slope that can lead to destruction. Because of grace, we are able to choose life. In verse 18, a new word appears in Paul's argument that stands in sharp contrast to slavery. Paul tells us that we have been "set free" from sin.[1] We must willingly submit to God in order to find real freedom. Paul expects these believers to know and follow a "pattern of teaching." While grace is the agent of change in our lives, devoting ourselves to correct doctrine is an important task in the church. What we believe is just as important as what we do.

Create your own brief description of Paul's message in 6:19–23.

5. Romans 6:19–23[1, 2, 3]

_____

_____

_____

_____

_____

Discoveries

Let's summarize our discoveries from Romans 6.

1. The presence of grace does not mean we can sin with impunity and grace will cover it.

2. Being free from sin is a choice we can make with the power of Christ.

3. We choose our own master—sin, or God.

4. What we believe is important because it will affect how we act.

5. Holiness is less about what we do or don't do and more about being in active relationship with God in a way that changes our very character.

6. A holy life is a life lived in service to God for the sake of the world.

Choices and the Story of God

Whenever we read a biblical text, it is important to ask how the text we are reading relates to the rest of the Bible. Romans 6 is not the only place in the Bible where we are reminded about the reality of sin in our lives and the ability we have with the power of God to reject sin and live a holy life. **In the space provided below, write a short summary of how these characters experience the choice between life with God and a life enslaved to sin.**

1. Genesis 3:6–7

_____

_____

_____

_____

_____

2. 1 Samuel 2:12, 17–18, 22–26

_____

_____

_____

_____

3. Isaiah 6:1–8

_____

_____

_____

_____

_____

_____

If you have a study Bible, it may have references in a margin, a middle column, or footnotes that point to other biblical texts. You may find it helpful in understanding how the whole story of God ties together to look up some of those other scriptures from time to time.

4. Matthew 5:38–48

_____
_____
_____
_____
_____
_____
_____
_____
_____
_____

5. Luke 7:36–50

_____
_____
_____
_____
_____
_____
_____
_____
_____

6. Hebrews 6:1–12

_____
_____
_____
_____
_____
_____
_____
_____
_____
_____

Romans and Our World Today

When we consider the issues of dying to sin, choosing life in Christ, and living holy lives in Scripture and in our world, Romans 6 can become the lens through which we see ourselves, our world, and how God works in our world today.

1. Why is it easy to believe that grace gives us license to sin, and why does Paul say we should reject that temptation?

The ability to choose sin remains because we are still part of a broken world. We have the ability to be free from sin because of our participation in grace and cooperation with the Holy Spirit, opening ourselves to the wealth of God's resources. Grace is not a license to sin but an invitation to new life, free from the things that diminish and degrade. When we fail to participate, we cut ourselves off from the power that lifts us up from sin. We are not free from the philosophical remnants of Gnosticism today. When we proclaim that there is an inner "me" that is disconnected from the body, we are in the world of Gnosticism. Paul would reject this view. We are interconnected individuals of spirit, soul, and body. Any attempt to divide these undermines our Christian belief in bodily resurrection.

Following the above example, answer these questions about how we can understand ourselves, our world, and God's action in our world today.

2. When you hear the phase "died to sin," how does that look in a believer's life today?

3. What is the distinction between being unable to sin and being able not to sin? Why is it important?

_____

_____

_____

_____

_____

4. In what ways do our daily choices impact our ability to sin or live a life of holiness?

_____

_____

_____

_____

_____

5. When you hear the word "holy," what images come to mind?

_____

_____

_____

_____

_____

6. When holiness is described in terms of relationship to God, how does that change how we think about holiness?

_____

_____

_____

_____

_____

Invitation and Response

God's Word always invites a response. Think about the way the themes of sin, holiness, and choosing God speak to us today. How do they invite us to respond?

_____

_____

_____

_____

_____

_____

_____

_____

What is your evaluation of yourself based on any or all of the verses found in Romans 6?

_____

_____

_____

_____

_____

_____

_____

_____

_____

_____

_____

_____

_____

Holiness is being
filled with God.

ROMANS 7

Most ancient Jews lived in a world they saw filled with idolatry, immorality, and unfaithfulness. Thankfully, they had the law to serve as a guardrail to keep them where they should be. To them, the law was holy because it stood against the sin that was so prevalent. Paul has made a startlingly different argument here in Romans, stating that the law has not constrained sin but has actually aroused it; it has allowed sin to use the law to produce *more* trespasses.

In perhaps the most anguished, intimate chapter in all of Pauline literature, he describes in emotional detail how the law is usurped by sin. Instead of diminishing sin, it arouses sin to a greater extent, and has become the focal point for Jewish pride and presumption. Paul has a different role in mind for the law. It does not diminish but instead identifies sin.

WEEK 7, DAY 1

Absorb the passage in Romans 7 by reading it aloud several times until you become familiar with its verses, words, and phrases.

The Setting

As Paul moves into chapter 7, his argument will grow more complicated and much more personal. There is much at stake for him as he writes. Paul has said some provocative things already, such as that the Jews do not have an inside track in this new faith. He has also seemed to indicate that the law does not make people righteous but only increases the awareness of sin. Paul is not willing to abandon the law completely; instead, he wants to assign it a new role. He already hinted at the proper role for the law in chapter 5, but here in chapter 7 he will describe this role in detail.

The Message

Romans 7 is one of the most debated and controversial passages in the New Testament. The dispute revolves around the viewpoint of the "I" pronoun starting in verse 7. What is the religious experience of the person speaking? The potential answers to this question are divided. Are these words autobiographical about Paul, or is there another explanation? Is this a description about life before Christ as opposed to life after accepting Christ? Is it describing aspirations and our inability to achieve? Or is it describing two different types of Christian experience, where one attempts to follow the law versus a more mature, Spirit-led life in Christ?

These are important questions for any reader. Our goal should always be to read the text like the first readers did. In order to do this, we have to let go of our modern experiences and the presuppositions we bring to the text. Perhaps the key to this section is found in verses 1, 7, and 14. Paul has already written explicitly that this section is for those who know the law, and he follows up by opening each major section in verses 7 and 14 with the first-person-plural "we." Yes, Paul is writing autobiographically here—but not from an individual perspective. Paul is writing as a representative of all who seek to live according to the law and, as a result, draw closer to God. This attempt proved to be a failure for him as a Jew, and it will have the same result for any believer who seeks to do the same after coming to Christ.

To discover the message of Romans 7, let's examine the passage by dividing it into four sections. **Summarize or paraphrase the general message or theme of each section (following the pattern provided).**

1. Romans 7:1–6

Paul makes it clear in this very first verse of the chapter that he is speaking to the Jewish Christians, and perhaps even Jewish believers who aren't fully on board yet with this new faith. He is using what they have in common—the law and traditions of Judaism—to remind them that he can be trusted because he is one of them.

What else do you see Paul saying in this section?

_____

_____

_____

2. Romans 7:7–13

_____

_____

_____

_____

_____

_____

3. Romans 7:14–20

_____

_____

_____

_____

_____

_____

4. Romans 7:21–25

_____

_____

_____

_____

_____

What's Happening in the Passage?

As we read through these passages there are certain ideas and words that were familiar to the original readers but are not as familiar to us. Two thousand years and a vastly different culture obscure some of these ideas from us today. You may encounter some of these words and ideas in your study today. Some of them have been explained in more detail in the **Word Study Notes** below. If you want even more detail you can supplement this study with a Bible dictionary or commentary.

1. Romans 7:1-6

In chapter 7 Paul picks up the argument from chapter 5, where he said that the effect of the law was to make sin even more sinful. Always anticipating the possible objections, Paul launches into a lengthy answer to the unasked question of whether the law is really sinful. Paul is speaking primarily to the Jewish believers, but also to gentiles who may have been attracted to the idea of keeping the law as a means of attaining righteousness. Paul refers to specific regulations within the Jewish law that release a wife from certain demands upon the death of her husband.[1] New believers choose to participate not only in the death of Christ but also in the death of their former way of living.[2] The imagery of baptism is helpful here. This visual proclamation of faith shows the willing death of the former life of every believer, and our rising again to new life in Christ.

WORD STUDY NOTES #1

[1] Paul is using the illustration of this example from the law to create an analogy. The Jewish believers were "married" to the law, and obligated to its demands. Death (to sin, through Christ) has released them from those obligations, just like the death of a husband would release a wife from the obligations to her marriage.

[2] The Greek word translated "you also died," *ethanatothete*, is in the passive voice and is best translated "you were put to death." In Greek, the passive voice is often used to indicate the action of God. So Paul is suggesting that God is responsible for bringing a fitting end to our former way of life.

2. Romans 7:7-13

Paul starts here by once again stating an anticipated objection to what he has been saying about the law—if the law produces sin, then the law must be sinful. Paul says absolutely not! Then he says the primary role of the law is to identify sin and educate the person who is aware of the law. If it hadn't been for the law, we would not even know what it means to covet. Paul is not saying covetous desires are not present in the world; he is saying that he (and other Jewish believers) didn't have a name for what those sins were, so they didn't know they were sins.[1] The law names coveting and informs us that it stands outside of God's expectation. The problem is that, once we know what it is, we inexplicably now have the desire to do the very thing the law forbids.[2] Yet Paul wants to assert that there is still value in knowing the standard. If we do not know what sin is, how will we know we need the Spirit? For this reason, Paul confidently asserts that the law is "holy, righteous and good."

WORD STUDY NOTES #2

[1] Remember that Paul's use of "I" follows his use of "we." He uses "we" to indicate to his audience that he is addressing every person who seeks to express faith by following the demands of law, believing it will give them some advantage. He uses "I" to help them identify with his own experience as a Jew learning about proper relationship to the law.

[2] Think about a child who is unaware there are cookies in the kitchen until they are told they cannot have any of the cookies that are in the kitchen. They didn't want them previously, but now that they know the cookies are there, and have been told they can't have them, cookies are their one and only desire.

WORD STUDY NOTES #3

[1] Paul's anguished emotional state is evident in these verses. When our desire is to fulfill the law, we fail to accomplish what we really wish to do. It is impossible without the grace of Christ and the indwelling presence of the Holy Spirit.

[2] Paul has discovered that performance of the law cannot fulfill God's purpose. The law's purpose is to identify sin, not create righteousness. That is why Paul can still call the law good.

[3] Remember that the type of slavery that Paul refers to is not the kind we are used to thinking about in the modern world. In Paul's world, slavery was a paid position. People entered the condition of slavery ("belonging" to another) in order to pay a debt, usually over a set period of time. When we view Paul's comparison of life in Christ to the ancient Roman system of slavery, we can better understand Paul's meaning: we are in great debt to the One who gave his life for us—a debt we will never be able to repay. Therefore, we "belong" to Christ for life.

104

Create your own brief summary or description of the reality portrayed in verses 14–20.

3. Romans 7:14–20[1, 2, 3]

4. Romans 7:21-25

The final note of despair for those who seek meaning by observing the law is sounded at the end of chapter 7, and the despair is total. Paul admits the possibility of good motives. The person living by the law can delight in trying to do good and having a relationship restored through external obedience. Even though the effort may be great, there is another power that undermines us at every turn. It is not enough to try to be obedient to the law. It is not even enough to succeed in getting every rule correct. The defeat is so total that Paul states there is another law at work—the power and presence of sin. Paul's emotional cry in verse 24 is a fitting response to what he has learned about the spiral of death that occurs when we are trapped in sin. At this point, the audience may be feeling Paul's despair right along with him, but there is a ray of light. What is the answer to our despair? "Thanks be to God—through Jesus Christ our Lord!"[1] To be continued . . .

WORD STUDY NOTES #4

[1] "Thanks be to God" is wonderful but incomplete. Paul has yet to explain how Jesus Christ fully answers the problem that Paul has outlined in such detail. He will offer this explanation in chapter 8.

Discoveries

Let's summarize our discoveries from Romans 7.

1. Because of Christ's work of death and resurrection, we are no longer obligated (or bound) to the laws of sin and death but have freedom in Jesus.

2. Sin is a powerful force that can tempt us in ways we never knew we could be tempted.

3. Performative faith cannot replace a living and active relationship with God.

4. Belonging to Christ, rather than to sin, changes how we think and what we do.

If you have a study Bible, it may have references in a margin, a middle column, or footnotes that point to other biblical texts. You may find it helpful in understanding how the whole story of God ties together to look up some of those other scriptures from time to time.

Death to Sin and the Story of God

Whenever we read a biblical text, it is important to ask how the text we are reading relates to the rest of the Bible. Romans 7 is not the only place in the Bible where we are reminded about the depths of sin in our lives and the possibility of new life in Christ after putting sin to death. **In the space provided below, write a short summary of how our experience with sin is navigated in these other passages.**

1. Ephesians 2:1–10

_____

_____

_____

_____

_____

_____

_____

_____

_____

2. Colossians 2:13–23

_____

_____

_____

_____

_____

_____

_____

_____

_____

3. 1 John 2:1–14

4. Hebrews 9:11–28

WEEK 7, DAY 5

Romans and Our World Today

Paul hits many of the same themes over and over in Romans, but with different nuances. When we consider the issues of dying to sin and choosing life in Christ in Scripture and in our world today, Romans 7 can become the lens through which we see ourselves, our world, and how God works in our world today.

1. When have you observed a situation where knowledge of a law or rule actually produced a desire to rebel against it?

_____

_____

_____

_____

_____

_____

2. Where have you experienced that temptation to rebel against rules in the Christian life?

_____

_____

_____

_____

_____

_____

3. What are some expectations or requirements that you have learned through the Bible or the teachings of the church?

_____

_____

_____

_____

_____

_____

_____

4. Why is it so hard to do the good thing even after identifying it as the good choice?

_____

_____

_____

_____

_____

_____

5. How does knowledge of the law change the character of sin to something more serious?

_____

_____

_____

_____

_____

_____

_____

Invitation and Response

God's Word always invites a response. Think about the way the theme of dying to sin and rising to new life in Christ speaks to us today. How does it invite us to respond?

_____

_____

_____

_____

_____

_____

_____

_____

_____

_____

_____

_____

What is your evaluation of yourself based on any or all of the verses in Romans 7?

_____

_____

_____

_____

_____

_____

_____

_____

_____

_____

_____

_____

_____

_____

Performative faith
cannot replace a
living and active
relationship with God.